Charles G.D. Roberts
and The Influence of His Times

CHARLES G.D. ROBERTS

and

The Influence

of

His Times

by
James Cappon

The Tecumseh Press
Ottawa, Canada
1975

ISBN 0-919662-53-6

The Tecumseh Press
8 Mohawk Crescent
Ottawa
Canada

Printed and bound in Canada

CONTENTS

I.–LITERARY WORLD OF TO-DAY

MR. ROBERTS has been before the public as a poet for about a quarter of a century. During that time some six or seven volumes of verse have come from his hands, and in 1901 a general collection of his poems was published in one volume. In a prefatory note to this last volume he tells us that it contains everything he cares to preserve of the poetry he had written before the end of 1898. To this he has recently added a small volume, *The Rose of Life*, so that the reader will find in those two books all that the poet himself cares to give him, or would like to be judged by.

But though Mr. Roberts is so well known by name to the public, and is certainly the most distinguished of our Canadian poets, of those, at any rate, who use the English language, it cannot be said that his poetry has taken any wide or deep hold of the Canadian people. In fact, with the exception of a sonnet or two which appear regularly in the new anthologies, it is doubtful if the poetry of Roberts is at all well known outside of a limited circle of readers mostly professional or semi-professional in their relation to literature. Some of these struggle valiantly to keep alive a languid public interest on the subject of Canadian poetry and poets by warm eulogies in the magazines or highly optimistic utterances at literary conferences. But literary conferences can do nothing to create a public interest in poetry which the poetry itself has failed to excite. As often as not the indiscriminate and universal eulogy which one hears at such gatherings, or reads in perfunctory reviews of Canadian literature, only dulls and confuses the public mind and leaves it with some very reasonable suspicion as to the value of poetry and higher literature in general. It is a very different kind of seed that must be sown before the great new democracies of to-day will show as lively and as critical an interest in these things as the aristocratic and aristocratically trained societies of the past did. What we need is not a blare of trumpets and loud proclamations that "Canada has a literature," or a "Burns" or a "Tennyson," but a candid and reverent criticism that will show the true value of imaginative literature and the part it is playing, nobly or ignobly, for it can do both, in our general life.

It is quite true that some forms of literature now receive a more generous support from the public than they ever did before. The modern novelist, for example, has an immense and indulgent public in the hosts of those who have money and leisure and are willing to amuse themselves with a story when they are not at the theatre or playing "bridge." The modern magazine writer and journalist also has a public which has converted ancient Grub Street into one of the opulent and respected quarters of the earth. Better still, it is true that poetry of a really first-rate quality in its kind has as large an audience as it ever had, whether it be the highly critical poetry of Browning or the popular lyric of Kipling. The poetry of Omar Khayyam, for example, which has had the good luck to be so translated in the curiously appropriate rhythms of Fitzgerald that even to the common ear it has become the perfect expression of one great chord in life, goes everywhere, watering like a hidden brook the dusty ways of the everyday world. The Rubaiyat is read, as Macandrew's Hymn is read, by those who care little in general for poetry. But there are other forms of literature which have almost suffered eclipse under our new democracies, at least on this side of the Atlantic. The old literary reviewer, for instance, has a poor time amongst us, I am afraid. The days when an article on Milton or Dr. Johnson made a sensation amongst the reading public are gone by. The modern reviewer must compress what he has to say into a five-page article; he must avoid literary and philosophic breadth of treatment and raise only issues which can be explained in a paragraph; or he must hide himself away in the

2

limbo of the philosophical reviews. It is only in these now that one hears about Byron and Wordsworth.

Another literary personage whose importance has dwindled greatly in these modern times is the old type of minor poet, the successor, the follower of some great, established school of poetry, the author of odes, or epics, or dramas in their classical form. When one thinks of the place which such minor poets as Beattie and Rogers and Mrs. Hemans held in the world of their time, of the reverence their works inspired, and the way in which they impressed themselves on the culture of their age, one sees what a curious displacement of literary interests has accompanied the growth of democracy. The culture which the general reader of to-day seeks is quantitatively greater as regards information. He is quick-brained and has a wide range of sensibilit.y; he wants to know something about many things, about railroad transportation and fish hatcheries, about radio-activity and Japanese art, even a little about literature or the Middle-ages. But he does not value the kind of education which the reading of Cowper's Task or Byron's Childe Harold, or even Washington Irving's Sketch-Book might give him. His knowledge has not the ethical centre or the imaginative depth it used to have. *Harper's Monthly Magazine* would no longer dare, as it did in 1851, to reprint Goldsmith's *Traveller* in full or make up an issue mainly of articles on subjects like Washington Irving and the Poetry of William Cullen Bryant, and Extracts from the Conversation of Erasmus and Sir Thomas More about Plato. In many ways indeed the literary atmosphere of the *Harper's* of half a century ago is superior to that of the *Harper's* of to-day. There is an intellectual charm and repose about that old *Harper's*, a poise of judgment and an imaginative breadth which are lacking in its more modern representative. The imaginative quality of the illustrations in the latter; Elizabethan mansions and gardens, old Italian cities, and the ruined battlements of Chateau Galliard, with the rooks flying about them, does not quite make up for the want of a similar quality in the text.

The popular magazines have to adapt themselves, of course, to the taste of the greatest number of their readers. Perhaps they have largely absorbed the public which once gave popularity and vogue to the Beatties and Youngs of a past generation. They have absorbed it on one side while the interest in scientific and economic philosophy has absorbed it on the other. It requires a very solid habit of mind, indeed, to resist

3

the fascinating variety of the popular magazine of our day. No form of the popular taste but is admirably studied and catered for there. You get the latest economic estimates and the latest wonders of science, storiettes in five pages, interviews with statesmen (which do not as a rule amount to much), and with actresses (which amount to more, sociologically at least), the history of Rockefeller or of the Amalgamated Copper Company, and such piquant specialities as Professor Simon Newcomb's vision of the end of the world, or Professor Boyesen of Harvard's studies of types of beauty amongst chorus girls, with illustrations. If the reader has a craving for something more ideal, something in the higher regions of art and literature, the able editor knows how to administer an opiate in the form of a four-page article on Velasquez or the Barbizon school, or it may be on the frescoes of the Pisan Campo Santo, or on Peire Vidal, the Troubadour, the atmosphere of the age in such cases being given, not by the text, which is generally very poor in this respect, but by clever illustrations in three-colour prints. A critical interest in literature may be represented by a gossipy account of Tolstoi with a picture of him at work in the fields in his peasant's blouse, or perhaps by an interview with Sudermann, accompanied by a translation of a page or two of *Die Ehre* or *Im Zweilicht*.

And there is much in the way of information in the popular magazine that we cannot do without. Where else should we learn about the iniquities of American municipalities and the Standard Oil Company, unless the magazine editors endowed such research? How is the minor poet who once held the ear of his generation with his epic or ode, even if it was unread by the next, to compete with all that in our time? He loses faith in his art and begins to think it is an archaic tradition, and he probably ends by seeking the protection of some art coterie or taking shelter in that grand haven of refuge for distressed literary craft, journalism. If he has a ready pen for prose work he can keep himself comfortably afloat there, and achieve a bye-reputation in one or the other department of literature. What may happen to the poet within him is another question. He may grow, as Henley did, into a wild Villon-like grace and defiant candour of utterance (with a touch of Alsatian swagger in it too, the Bilbo trailing conspicuously at his heels); or he, the poet, may die in the very opulence of modern Grub Street, or because of the over-mastering spell of Vagabondia, while the man is still alive and publishing quatrains in praise of Omar or *vers libre* in praise of life.

But whatever position the minor poet may occupy in the varied intellectual activity of our time, when he has produced such a notable quantity of work as Roberts has, work representing a strenuous and singularly varied effort at the poetic interpretation of life, his career can hardly fail to be an interesting document in the history of his country and his age. It is not always in the great master that you can read most clearly the character of the time. The great master has a way of sublimating into greatness all the intellectual tendencies of the age, and even its conceits and affectations, as Shakespeare, for example, can make the euphuism and exaggerated emphasis of the Elizabethan period pass muster with us. But in the minor poet you can examine characteristic modes of thought and forms of art with a steadier and less dazzled eye. If you want to understand the standards of the eighteenth century in verse you should look at the poetry of Garth and Addison as well as at that of Pope and Goldsmith.

II.–EARLY POEMS–THE SCHOOL OF KEATS. ACTAEON.

IT is natural for a young poet to begin by following some established tradition in his art, and Roberts started with one of the highest. The direct influence of Keats had almost ceased to be felt in English poetry when the Canadian poet revived it in its purest form for his countrymen. His early poems hardly disguise the fact that they are imitations of Keats, and belong to that new world of Arcadia which the English poet had created. That poetic world which Crabbe and Wordsworth, with their naturalism, thought they had banished; that land where the departed gods and heroes of Hellas still live, where the steps of Pan are still heard in the forest, and Thetis glides with silvery feet over the waves, had been revived for us by the poet of Endymion, and its green bowers had allured a good many poetic aspirants into them, amongst whom Roberts may be counted as the latest, perhaps the last. For the poetry of to-day is looking for its material in another region where the forms of life are more robust and actual and the atmosphere more electrical than they are in the old legendary world of Arcadia.

From a philosophic point of view, there was nothing very complete in Keats' reconstruction of the Greek mythology. But he gave it all that poetry needs to make a new world of, a new sky, a new earth and new seas enchanting as those of fairyland;

he filled its landscape with green wealth and aerial minstrelsy and every harmonious form of beauty in shape or sound or colour. But, more than all, he created the language in which alone this new world could be fitly described, a new language of idyllic description, a language of the subtlest, impressionistic power which could render the shapes of things seen in this dreamland with a visionary distinctness altogether unique. Its movement and cadence, too, were unique, natural as those of a man talking to himself, yet quaint and captivating as voices from the cave of the Sibyl:

> 'Twas a lay
> More subtle-cadenced, more forest wild
> Than Dryope's lone lulling of her child;
> And nothing since has floated on the air
> So mournful strange.

If Southey had been able to discover a similar language for his Domdaniels and Padalons his grandiose epics would not be where they now are, but that would be saying that Southey had a poetic genius which he had not. The line of Keats was a marvellous creation, and made him the indispensable master for all the idyllic poets who came after him. He had the master's secret of making everything which he touched new. His Apollos and Naiads had nothing to do with the fossilised mythology of the eighteenth century poets; you never thought of comparing them; you never thought of his "leaden-eyed despairs" in connection with the deliberate personifications of Collins or Gray, no more than you thought of the stiff framework of the eighteenth century couplet in reading his fluent verse.

Of course there was something in his style which remains inimitable and his own. The imaginative felicity of his phrase, the passionate simplicity of his cry, the entire naturalness of his movement, no one could repeat these. But there was also something which could be more or less easily imitated, and this became the possession of a whole school, and even part of the universal language of poetry. That large, elusive epithet, that new reach of synecdoche, those novel compounds, that richly blazoned phrase in general, with delicate luxury and efflorescence, were readily appropriated by the aesthetic schools of poetry. Phrases like "argent revelry," "warm-cloistered hours," "tall oaks branch-charmed by the earnest stars," set the mould for a new and finely sensuous impressionism in descriptive poetry. The critics of *Blackwood* and the *Quarterly* might sniff

7

at first at the new poesy as the sickly affectation of the Cockney School, but it could not long be neglected by young poets seeking to learn the secrets of colour and rhythm in their art. The youthful Tennyson quietly drew some of his finest threads for his own loom, and Rossetti, with the whole aesthetic school, shows everywhere the influence of Keats' line. To most of them he was more even than Shelley, for he taught them more, though the other, with the star-domed grandeur of his universe, and his Titanic passion and conflict might be the greater inspiration to them. William Rossetti says of his famous brother that he "truly preferred" Keats to Shelley, "though not without some compunctious visitings now and then."

As to Wordsworth's influence, it is not surprising that there is little or no trace of it in the early work of Roberts, though it was just the time when the reputation of the sage and singer of Rydal Mount was in its second bloom with the public, owing mainly to the fine and discriminating criticism of Arnold. But the young poets of the aesthetic school disliked Wordsworth. They hated the plain texture of his style and its want of colour. It might, however, have been well for Roberts if he had come under the influence of Wordsworth's simplicity and candour at this formative period of his life.

But, for better or worse, the school of Keats was that in which Mr. Roberts received his training. He simply lives at this period in that green world of neo-classical idyllism which Keats had created. The style of the master, his colour, his rhythmical movement, his manner of treating his subject, are reproduced with the interesting, but somewhat deceptive similitude which a copy always gives of a great original. In the *Ode to Drowsihood* we hear the well-known lyrical cry:

> Ah! fetch thy poppy baths, juices exprest
> In fervid sunshine, where the Javan palm
> Stirs, scarce awakened from its odorous calm
> By the enervate wind,

and in the stanzas of the *Ariadne* almost every epithet and every verb recall something which is familiar to us in the manner of the master:

> Hung like a rich pomegranate o'er the sea
> The ripened moon; along the tranced sand
> The feather-shadowed ferns drooped dreamfully,
> The solitude's evading harmony

8

Mingled remotely over sea and land;
A light wind woke and whispered warily,
   And myriad ripples tinkled on the strand.

That poetry is steeped in the rich Tyrian dye of Keats' fancy,
and the luxury of sense impression which is so marked in the
work of the master is the too exclusive quality of the disciple's.
For after all there is an ethical element in the poetry of Keats
which Roberts does not reproduce so well, an insistence on the
spirituality and the healthfulness of beauty which runs through
all the work of the English poet and gives its special flavour
to many of his finest passages. It is the ascetic element needed
to complete the chord in Keats, without which his poetry
would be rather overpowering in its sensuous richness. Every
one knows the opening lines of Endymion and the fine
outburst in *The Ode to a Grecian Urn*:

Heard melodies are sweet, but those unheard
   Are sweeter; therefore, ye soft pipes, play on;
Not to the sensual ear, but, more endeared,
   Pipe to the spirit ditties of no tone.

The epic of *Orion*, Mr. Roberts' most ambitious effort,
though he preserves only a fragment of it in the one volume
edition of his poems, also belongs to this early period. The
material is still that of the Keatsian idyll, a romantic treatment
of mythical Greek figures, sylvan deities, Arcadian shepherd
kings, with a luxurious impressionistic treatment of Arcadian
landscape as its background. The style is often highly affected:

And now it was about the set of sun,
And the west sea-line with its quivering rim
Had hid the sun-god's curls.

In the descriptive parts the line is too often burdened with
epithets, the search for aesthetic picturesque material taking
up the energy which might go into deeper forms of characterisation:

For there the deep-eyed night
Looked down on me; unflagging voices called
From unpent waters falling; tireless wings
Of long winds bare me tongueless messages
From star-consulting, silent pinnacles;
And breadth, and depth, and stillness fathered me.

So *Orion* discourses. Allow for the remote lengendary

9

atmosphere of the tale and the manner in which the mysterious converse of a demi-god with the ancient elemental voices of mother earth must be communicated, that style is still a hollow and overwrought form; it depends almost entirely on a vague impressionism which does not succeed in fixing truly the imaginative shape of the things swimming in its vision. This inchoate, formless character of the imaginative power is easily felt in the epithets which are so pretentious and yet express so little intimate or real experience.

It could hardly be otherwise. The poem of *Orion* is grandiose and empty because the young poet is moving in a world at once too vast and too attenuated in the forms of its life to be treated on this epic scale. It needed the overflowing imagination of a Keats to fill that world with the contours and colours of life suitable to it, with deities and piping fauns, with naiads and shepherds, rural festivals and choral hymns, and all the legendary motley of Arcadia. It needed all the magic of his style and his exquisite touch in nature description to overcome its huge artificiality. Even in him its main interest and only underlying reality was the idyllic representation of nature which he could blend so happily with that old Greek symbolism. His Arcadian personages, although there are brilliant traits in their make-up, stand for nothing.

After *Orion* Roberts seems to have felt some decay of the impulse towards classical mythological themes. He had celebrated his entry into the region of Arcadian song in a characteristically high and jubilant strain:

Surely I have seen the majesty and wonder
    Beauty, might and splendour of the soul of song;
Surely I have felt the spell that lifts asunder
    Soul from body, when lips faint and thought is strong.

Anche io son poeta! But now, in *Iterumne*, he seems to breathe a mournful farewell to Arcadian legend. The breeze, he complains, is no longer blowing from Thessalian Tempe and the swift Peneus, no vision of goddess or Dryad comes to him any more:

Ah me! No wind from golden Thessaly
    Blows in on me as in the golden days;
    No morning music from its dew-sweet ways,
No pipings, such as came so clear to me
Out of green meadows by the sparkling sea;
    No goddess any more, no Dryad strays,

10

And glorifies with songs the laurel maze;
Or else I hear not and I cannot see.

For out of weary hands is fallen the lyre,
    And sobs in falling; all the purple glow
    From weary eyes is faded, which before
Saw bright Apollo and the blissful choir
    In every mountain grove. Nor can I know
    If I shall surely see them anymore.

Very weary, surely, are the hands and eyes of one-and-twenty! But some reaction from the first ecstasy of young inspiration was natural, and the poet may already have begun to feel some shrinking and fading in that Arcadian world of his fancy. Probably also he was beginning to suspect that the temper of the age was not so favourable to that remote visionary treatment of life as it once had been. Besides, although the character of Mr. Roberts' talent is decidedly of the high traditional literary kind, he has also, as one may see from his later career, strong popular instincts, and he would soon realise that to reach any wide public in Canada he must choose themes with more of the actual life and interests of to-day in them.

But though Mr. Roberts after this period began to seek a less remote kind of subject for his song, he has never altogether deserted the old fields of Greek legend. From time to time the wind blows again from Thessalian Tempe and brings us a strain or two of the old music. Indeed, *Actaeon*, which was published in 1887 in the volume *In Divers Tones*, is Roberts' most successful achievement in the region of classical idyll. But the manner in which he treats his subject is no longer that of Keats and his school, not purely at least. He combines it with a dramatic monologue in that psychological style which Browning has made so familiar to us. The subject of the poem is the story of Actaeon's death, but it is told by "a woman of Plataea," who is supposed to have witnessed the tragedy, and is converted by it from scepticism to fear the gods. The first part of the poem, in which the Plataean woman tells the story of her own life, is modelled in some extent on the close, tense, psychological movement of Browning, and his realistic manner of presenting his personages in dramatic monologue. Even the style at times has familiar touches, a curt emphasis and rough, dramatic cuts in the verse, which remind us of Browning; though, on the whole, it is Tennysonian, spun out of the mingled simplicity and ornateness of Tennyson's diction. The second part of the poem, in which the woman tells the story

11

of Actaeon's death, is wholly descriptive, the material being legendary idyllic, and treated in the smooth, remote manner natural to the Arcadian idyll.

Here are some lines from the introductory part, in which the Plataean woman discourses on the nature of the gods. You can see the brusque jets of Browning's manner mingling with the more languid and musical phrase of Tennyson. The psychology is very simple, but there is a certain piquancy in this presentation of scepticism in a Greek dress:

I have lived long and served the god, and drawn
Small joy and liberal sorrow—scorned the gods,
And drawn no less my little meed of good,
Suffered my ill in no more grievous measure.

Ay, have I sung, and dreamed that they would hear,
And worshipped, and made offerings—it may be
They heard, and did perceive, and were well pleased—
A little music in their ears, perchance,
A grain more savor to their nostrils, sweet
Tho' scarce accounted of. But when for me
The mists of Acheron have striven up,
And horror was shed round me; when my knees
Relaxed, my tongue clave speechless, they forgot.
And when my sharp cry cut the moveless night,
And days and nights my wailings clamoured up
And beat about their golden homes, perchance
They shut their ears. No happy music this,
Eddying through their nectar cups and calm!
Then I cried out against them, and died not;
And rose and set me to my daily tasks.
So all day long, with bare, uplift right arm,
Drew out the strong thread from the carded wool,
Or wrought strange figures, lotus-buds and serpents,
In purple on the himation's saffron fold;
Nor uttered praise with the slim-wristed girls
To any god, nor uttered any prayer.

There are some fine natural traits in the picture of the Plataean woman, and, on the whole, she is the most life-like of the few human figures, mythical or modern, that appear in Roberts' poems. But she is strangely out of place in the atmosphere of a mythus. Her personality and speech have the realistic accent of a historic time, and refuse absolutely to blend with the figures of a mythopoetic age which witnessed the metamorphosis of Actaeon and saw the gods of Olympus walking on the earth. There are two different atmospheres in the poem fundamentally discordant with each other, and the manner in which the poet connects the two is at best an ingenious artifice without psychological truth or significance. But though the psychological basis of the poem is weak, it has its merits as a tale told fluently and with a certain subtlety of art. It has, too, in the latter part a fine background of descriptive impressionism such as the legendary idyll requires:

> Cithaeron, bosomed deep in soundless hills,
> Its fountained vales, its nights of starry calm,
> Its high, chill dawns, its long-drawn, golden days.

The description of the "homeless pack" is good, and that closing touch about the wind that blows down on them and dies away in the dark—an aesthetic consonance of nature covering her huge, elemental indifference towards human fate—shows the delicate sensibility of the poet in this direction.

Off Pelorus is another excursion into the region of classical legend, and illustrates the artistic variety of Mr. Roberts' experiments in moulds and metres. It tells the old tale of Ulysses and the Sirens in a manner which combines the characteristic qualities of two or three of the great poets of the aesthetic and impressionistic schools, the romantic and almost effeminate treatment which Tennyson gives classical legend, the luxurious warmth of phrase and the fulness of picturesque detail which one finds in some poems of Keats's, and the passionate, lyrical movement, heightened by alliterative emphasis, which is characteristic of Swinburne.

> Crimson swims the sunset over far Pelorus:
>> Burning crimson tops its frowning crest of pine.
> Purple sleeps the shore and floats the wave before us,
>> Eachwhere from the oar-stroke eddying warm like wine.

The measure actually used, however, is that of Browning in the *Epilogue to Ferishstah's Fancies*, with the omission of a foot in the second and fourth lines of the stanza, which shortens its majestic stride and lowers the heroic cadences slightly. That "eachwhere" represents a certain recklessness characteristic of Roberts, and so does, in a still deeper way, the violent expedient by which he manages to introduce the Siren's song. He makes the sailors *guess* its words from the expressive struggle of Ulysses to free himself from his bonds.

On the whole, we cannot rate very highly this Greek legen-

dary element in the poetry of Roberts. It needs an utter perfection of style and a fancy of exquisite delicacy to wake these old and very decayed chords in the history of our civilisation into life again. The highly cultivated interest in literature which welcomes such productions as the *Endymion*, or Aubrey de Vere's *Lycius* and Swinburne's *Atalanta*, is confined to a comparatively small class, and it must be a masterpiece in this species of poetry that a busy world is not very willing to let die. It takes the supreme art of a Virgil and a Milton to repeat the cry of the Daphnis song, "O Pan, Pan," with anything like success, and only the imaginative power of a Keats can charm us into thinking that we feel once more the underlying realities of that old Arcadian nature-worship. For it had a certain reality as a mode of interpreting the vague voices that come from nature to man, and poetry like that of Keats had a power of putting us into some vital contact with its ancient pieties. But anything less genuine is apt to be a mere academic exercise which gives us only an artificial and obsolete framework to look at. The *Lycidas* and the *Lamia* do not grow old or out of fashion, but who speaks of the *Lycius* or the *Search After Proserpine* now? Mr. Roberts plays sweetly enough on his "shepherd's pipe of Arcady." His melodies were learned in the finest school of that art and he shows a wonderful facility in absorbing the finest tones and hues of the school and giving them forth again in moulds which have a certain novelty, yet just lack the stamp of true originality. There is a strain of medley, too, in his song which old Palaemon should have detected and checked. But he, I think, is drowsing in these times, and has fallen into his old fashion of lazily bestowing the heifer on all comers: *Et vitula tu dignus, et hic, et quisquis.*
. . .

III.–POETRY OF NATURE. TANTRAMAR REVISITED

THE training which Roberts received in the school of Keats was mainly that of a nature poet. The underlying reality in the neo-classical idyll was its beautiful, if rather fanciful, treatment of nature, which was based, just as that of the ancient idyll had been, on a free selection of all fine pastoral images untramelled by conditions of climate or locality. The poet might revel in any combinations of scenery which his imagination suggested as long as he could give the whole the harmony which here took the place of reality. The oceans might be as serene and the Arcadian hunting ranges as wild as he liked:

> With muffled roarings through the clouded night,
> And heavy splashings through the misty pools.

Of course he had chosen the school because it gave a splendid form to his own natural instincts as a poet. His real power, his original impulse towards poetry, lies nearly altogether in the region of nature description, and it was a short and natural step for him to take from the fanciful delineations of nature in *Orion* and *Actaeon* to the description of actual Canadian scenes. But it involved in his case a decided change in the forms of poetic composition. The grand framework of epic and idyllic narrative, which he could use when he had that shad-

15

owy Arcadian mythology to fill it with the shapes of life, was laid aside. We have no modern idylls like Goethe's *Hermann and Dorothea* or Tennyson's *Enoch Arden* from him. So also the large framed 7 or 9 line pentameter stanza, and the strophe of Keats, with its rich rhyme and the long cadences which murmured of 'old Cretan melodies' or the Javan palm, give place to light, popular quatrains and couplets and the half lawless structure of the short-line stanza. It was a change which had already taken place very generally in the poetry of our time, as part of that return to nature and simplicity of form which had begun with Wordsworth. Our new singers seem no longer willing to support the weight of those grand forms of stanzaic verse which the great poets of the Italian Renaissance and all those who followed their traditions loved so well. The sonnet, with its well-established paces, is about the only great traditional form in use now.

It is a kind of light lyrical and descriptive verse which is the most characteristic form of Roberts' productivity at this period. Pleasant little snatches of song like *Birch and Paddle, On the Creek, A Song of Cheer, Aylesford Lake, The Brook in February, An August Wood Road, In the Afternoon*; charming glimpses of Canadian scenery, with a general simplicity of style and trait which recalls the old lyrical school of Longfellow and Whittier:

Afar from stir of streets,
    The city's dust and din,
What healing silence meets
    And greets us gliding in!

Our light birch silent floats;
    Soundless the paddle dips.
Yon sunbeam thick with motes
    Athro' the leafage slips.

That is from *Birch and Paddle. Aylesford Lake*, however, has more of the silvery cadence and smooth workmanship of Tennyson:

All night long the light is lying
    Silvery on the birches sighing,
All night long the loons are crying
    Sweetly over Aylesford Lake.

The Solitary Woodsman, a little idyll of Canadian life which

16

haunts the mind after you have read it, as true poetry will, may be noticed here, although it was published at a later time in *The Book of the Native* (1897). The Woodsman represents nearly all that Roberts has given us in the way of human portraiture,* and even his personality, it must be admitted, is of the faintest. But there is a beautiful simplicity and naturalness about the poem.

All day long he wanders wide
With the grey moss for his guide,
    And his lonely axe-stroke startles
The expectant forest side.

Toward the quiet close of day
Back to camp he takes his way
    And about his sober footsteps
Unafraid the squirrels play.

On his roof the red leaf falls,
At his door the blue jay calls,
    And he hears the wood mice hurry
Up and down his rough log-walls:

Hears the laughter of the loon
Thrill the dying afternoon,—
    Hears the calling of the moose
Echo to the early moon.

It needed only a touch more to make that solitary woodsman as universal and popular a portrait as Longfellow's *Village Blacksmith*, a touch more of personal detail and moral characterisation. A contemplative delicacy of feeling for nature is the chief characteristic of the poems of this class and they are best when they remain simply descriptive.

In many of these poems Mr. Roberts has gone back both in style and sentiment to the older and simpler schools of lyrical poetry so different in their naive tunefulness and gay movement from the poets of to-day with their heavily essenced verse and deliberate mysticism. There are airs from Herrick in him as well as from Tennyson. At times he even gives us popular lyrics, true folk-rhythms like *The Stack Behind the Barn* or *In the Barn-Yard's Southerly Corner*, mostly modelled on old English lilts, with catching refrains. These belong to that poetry of tender reminiscence, memories of boyhood, the pathetic note of which has often been struck so truly by our

17

*Of course there are the ballads with a few figures in them slightly touched. But ballad poetry of this kind is a naive and archaic form of presenting life which does not properly come into question here.

minor singers. You can hear the true note of it in the forgotten poetry of Miss Blamire as well as in Burns or in Heine's *Mein Kind, wir waren Kinder*:

> To wean me frae these woefu' thoughts
>> They took me to the toun:
> But sair on ilka weel-kenned face
>> I missed the youthfu' bloom.

> At balls they pointed to a nymph
>> Wham a' declared divine:
> But sure her mother's blushing cheeks
>> Were fairer far langsyne.

Roberts is vigorous and picturesque enough in his barn-yard lilts and occasionally catches a fine refrain

> Oh, merrily shines the morning sun
> In the barn-yard's southerly corner.

But he wants the soft note and ingenuous simplicity proper to this kind of poetry. There is almost too much vigour of accent and too evident a determination in the accumulation of details:

> Dear memory of the old home farm—
> The hedge-rows fencing the crops from harm;
> The cows, too heavy with milk for haste;
> The barn-yard, yellow with harvest waste
>> And the stack behind the barn.

Indeed I hardly think this plaintive note is so natural to the age or the country as it was to the Doric songs of old Scotland. The weight of the past does not lie so heavily, so pathetically, on our eager and aspiring democracies.

Amongst all these varieties of the Canadian idyll, the one which leaves the strongest impression on the mind of originality in tone and treatment is *Tantramar Revisited*. Here Roberts' classical taste in style again asserted itself, though in the not very pure form of the modern hexameter. Longfellow had given the measure popular currency on this continent in his *Evangeline*, and Mathew Arnold had lately been directing the attention of literary circles to its possibilities. Both he and the poet Clough had done something to rescue it from the monotonous softness of Longfellow's movement and give it more strength and variety. Roberts, who has never quite lost his first love for the grand style, was quick to profit by the lesson and uses this high but somewhat artificial form as a mould in which to pour his tenderest memories of the scenes familiar to his youth on the coast of New Brunswick. There is no direct picture of life in the poem, not a single human figure, but the landscape is powerfully painted in large, distant, softened traits, the true colour of elegiac reminiscence. Of direct elegiac reflection the poet has been sparing, perhaps wisely, but what there is has a sincerity which shows how deeply he felt his subject.

Summers and summers have come and gone with the flight
of the swallow;
Sunshine and thunder have been, storm and winter and
frost;
Many and many a sorrow has all but died from
remembrance,
Many a dream of joy fall'n in the shadow of pain.

Hands of chance and change have marred, or moulded, or
broken,
Busy with spirit and flesh, all I have most adored;
Even the bosom of Earth is strewn with heavier shadows—
Only in these green hills, aslant to the sea, no change.

Yonder, toward the left, lie broad the Westmoreland
marshes,—
Miles and miles they extend, level, and grassy, and dim,
Clear from the long red sweep of flats to the sky in the
distance,
Save for outlying heights, green-rampired Cumberland
Point;
Miles on miles outrolled, and the river-channels divide
them,—
Miles on miles of green, barred by the hurtling gusts.

Now at this season the reels are empty and idle; I see them
Over the lines of the dykes, over the gossiping grass,
Now at this season they swing in the long strong wind
through the lonesome,
Golden afternoon, shunned by the foraging gulls.

Soon thro' their dew-wet frames, in the live keen freshness
of morning,
Out of the teeth of the dawn blows back the awakening
wind,

19

Then as the blue day mounts, and the low-shot shafts of the
   sunlight
Glance from the tide to the shore, gossamers jewelled with
   dew
Sparkle and wave, where late sea-spoiling fathoms of
   drift-net
Myriad-meshed, uploomed sombrely over the land,
Well I remember it all. The salt, raw scent of the margin;
While, with men at the windlass, groaned each reel, and the
   net,
Surging in ponderous lengths, uprose and coiled in its
   station;
Then each man to his home,—well I remember it all!

In spite of the exotic character of the verse, which after all
is a bar to the highest qualities of expression, something of the
visionary eye and depth of feeling with which the poet looks
on those scenes of his boyhood gets into every line. The poem
is a true whole also and speaks in a subtle way to the heart.
Perhaps he has lavished the resources of his style a little too
freely on that description of the empty net reels. Its luxuriance
is rather overpowering.

At the best this imitation of a classical measure is a strong
compelling mould which is apt to draw the poet into iterations
and to carry him further than he wishes at one time while
reining him up unduly at another. Mr. Roberts manages to use
it with some freedom and naturalness, but it is at the cost of
some rough lines, lines overloaded with awkward spondees or
technically impure and sometimes falling out of metre
altogether. This is particularly the case with the pentameter
variation which he uses, following Clough's example in
Amours de Voyage. It is designed of course to afford some
relief from the monotonously majestic stride of the hexameter
and allow the poet to escape into plainer cadences. Roberts
often uses it somewhat recklessly:

Stained with time, set warm in orchards, meadows and
   wheat.
or
Golden afternoon, shunned by the foraging gulls.

But often, too, he is the victor in the struggle that this
measure particularly excites between the metrical mould and
the natural idiom of language, as in that
Busy with spirit and flesh, all I have most adored.

IV.—SONGS OF THE COMMON DAY, A SONNET SEQUENCE. THE NEW POETIC DICTION

MR. ROBERTS has tried a great variety of tones and themes in the course of his poetic career; no poet so many, that I know of. But the deepest thing in his poetic passion and experience is his poetry of nature description. Its basis is, in general, a pure aestheticism, for though it may occasionally be mingled with some fanciful train of thought or have appended to it a Wordsworthian moral, its value lies wholly in the gleaming and glancing surface which it brings before the reader's eye. This impressionistic nature poetry is the best part of his old Keatsian heritage for one thing, and it is part perhaps of his best days also, the days he describes in *Tantramar Revisited*, long youthful days spent on the coast or amongst the farmsteads of New Brunswick, when he strove hardest to catch and to shape into some new line the vague, evasive, elemental beauty of nature. The power which he acquired then has never deserted him amongst all the transformations of spirit and literary ideals which he has experienced. Touches of it abound everywhere in his poems. He has always the glance and vision in this region. The task before him at this period, as he must have felt, was to find a high and complete form of expression for this power. This was not so easy, for, as one might guess from his general evasion of the subject except in some remote legendary form, he had little or no faculty for the direct

21

presentation of human life, and of itself this impressionistic power would hardly suffice to furnish forth an idyll or an elegy. He had done the feat once in *Tantramar Revisited*, but it could not easily be repeated. It was a happy inspiration, therefore, which made him think of putting his poetic impressions of Canadian pastoral life and scenery together in the form of a sonnet sequence. Some of these sonnets had been published earlier in an independent form, and were doubtless written without any thought of a sequence, but in 1892 they appeared as part of a collection under the title of *Songs of the Common Day*.

The Sonnet Sequence is a poetic form which unites a certain harmony of effect with entire independence in the treatment of each member of the series. It is a succession of short efforts with a continuity of aim which is capable of producing in the end something of the effect of a great whole. It has the authority of great literary traditions from Petrarch to Wordsworth, and it seems to be nearly the only grand form of composition which the poetry of to-day can attempt with success. In this form then Mr. Roberts describes for us the general aspects of life and nature as one might see them at some Canadian farmstead, near the coast of New Brunswick, I suppose—spring pastures and summer pools, burnt lands and clearings, fir forests and the winter stillness of the woods, mingled with descriptions of the common occupations of farm life, milking time and mowing, the potato harvest, bringing home the cattle and the like, all in a kind of sequence from spring sowing to midwinter thaw.

The poet, I need hardly say, finds a splendid field here for the impressionistic glance and vision. Look at this description of a September afternoon:

A mystic rune
Foreboding the fall of summer soon,
Keeps swelling and subsiding; till there seems
O'er all the world of valley, hill and streams,
Only the wind's inexplicable tune.

Or at this, from the sonnet *Where the Cattle Come to Drink*:

The pensive afterthoughts of sundown sink
Over the patient acres given to peace;
The homely cries and farmstead noises cease,
And the worn day relaxes, link by link.

If these passages were found in Wordsworth, say in the series of sonnets on the Duddon, they would be quoted by everyone as fine and subtle renderings of the moods of nature. Another striking example of Roberts' gift in this direction is to be found in the last sonnet of the series, *The Flight of the Geese*. I shall quote it in full:

I hear the low wind wash the softening snow,
    The low tide loiter down the shore. The night,
    Full filled with April forecast, hath no light,
The salt wave on the sedge-flat pulses slow,
Through the hid furrows lisp in murmurous flow
    The thaw's shy ministers; and hark! The height
    Of heaven grows weird and loud with unseen flight
Of strong hosts prophesying as they go.

High through the drenched and hollow night their wings
    Beat northward hard on winter's trail.
        The sound
    Of their confused and solemn voices, borne
    Athwart the dark to their long arctic morn,
        Comes with a sanction and an awe profound,
A boding of unknown, foreshadowed things.

The purist might find fault with the strong lyrism of that sonnet and with inelegancies like that thrice repeated overflow from two final words of the same structure, but it is a splendid piece of imaginative impressionism and a fine example of Roberts' power of style in this field.

Many of these sonnets have a luxuriance of style and fancy, particularly in the direction of what Ruskin has called the Pathetic Fallacy, which is perhaps excessive for this poetic form with its small compass; but some of them also show a new plainness of style and treatment indicating that realistic influences from Wordsworth are beginning to work on Roberts. Sometimes there is even a kind of roughness in the manner of giving details, as in the following from *The Potato Harvest*:

Black on the ridge, against that lonely flush,
    A cart and stoop-necked oxen; ranged beside
    Some barrels; and the day-worn harvest folk,
Here emptying their baskets, jar the hush
    With hollow thunders. Down the dusk hillside
    Lumbers the wain; and day fades out like smoke.

The Furrow and *In an Old Barn* are also, in part at least,

23

examples of this closer, more realistic treatment. Here, too, I may notice *The Sower*, the poet's popular masterpiece, which hits the golden mean between austerity and luxuriance of style:

> A brown, sad-coloured hillside, where the soil,
>   Fresh from the frequent harrow, deep and fine,
>   Lies bare; no break in the remote skyline,
> Save where a flock of pigeons streams aloft,
> Startled from feed in some low-lying croft,
>   Or far-off spires with yellow of sunset shine;
>   And here the sower, unwittingly divine,
> Exerts the silent forethought of his toil.
>
> Alone he treads the glebe, his measured stride
>   Dumb in the yielding soil; and though small joy
>   Dwell in his heavy face, as spreads the blind,
> Pale grain from his dispensing palm aside,
>   The plodding churl grows great in his employ;
>   Godlike, he makes provision for mankind.

The selection and treatment of materials in that sonnet are perfect. It is equally free from unleavened realism of detail and from impressionistic finery, from those over-feathered shafts of phrase which hang so heavy on the thought in sonnets like *The Summer Pool* and *A Vesper Sonnet*. The traits are select, harmonious and firmly drawn, with a wise economy of stroke. The manner in which the eye is conducted from the solitary field to the distant horizon, where lies that world of men for whom the sower works, and then concentrated again on the scene of the sower's labour and his movements, is a good illustration of the simplicity and naturalness of a perfect piece of art. The closing thought is noble and true to the subject, reflecting itself powerfully back on the previous details in a way which gives them new significance.

Technically Mr. Roberts' sonnets generally show something of the structural freedom and something also of the looseness of conception which are characteristic of American sonnets. The rhyme system as a rule is the pure Petrarchan, but as often as not he entirely disregards the division of thought in the two quatrains of the octave. Sometimes the poise and counterpoise of thought between the octave and sestet is strongly marked, the first containing the descriptive part and the second the moral which the poet appends to it. At other times the division is but faintly felt, though it often exists in a form which is virtually a new type of sonnet structure. In this type the octave gives the general outline of a landscape and is followed by a sestet which gives a more particular description of some characteristic or significant object in it. This is the structural character of *The Herring Weir, The Oat Threshing, The Sower, The Flight of the Geese*, and other sonnets. In this way the old function of the sestet in summing up or pointing the significance of the octave is revived in a new form, and when the object thus selected for particular treatment is significant enough, and its connection with the description in the octave evident and inevitable, this arrangement makes an excellent type of sonnet. It is part of the perfection of *The Sower* that the connection between the landscape described in the octave and the object described in the sestet is of this natural, inevitable kind. But *The Sower* perhaps owes something of the selectness and harmony of its details to the fact that the subject is one which has been worked over by more than one great mind in the sister arts of painting and engraving. It is a curious example of the relation which may occasionally exist between poetry and the other fine arts, and Roberts may be counted fortunate in having furnished a perfect literary expression for a conception on which Durer and Millet had laboured.

On the whole this sonnet sequence may be considered as the most important poetic work Mr. Roberts has so far produced. It represents in its highest form what is most original in him, that in which his experience is deeper than that of other men. It gives the fairest scope, too, for that impressionistic painting of nature in which he is a master. The general tone of these sonnets is that of a pensive melancholy such as arises naturally enough from the contemplation of quiet pastoral morns and eves. Grey Corot-like pictures they mostly are, often a little huddled and indistinct or indeterminate in their outlines but delicately tinted and suffused with a true Canadian atmosphere of light and space and wide, pale, clear horizons. It is an atmosphere which keeps the colour tone of the landscape low, or at least cool, with nothing of tropical luxuriance about it, the bloom of the golden-rod, of the clover, the buttercups and the great purple patches of fire-weed in the woods being tempered by the cold clear lustre of a northern sky and the pale verdure of the marshes. The general features of nature in eastern Canada are faithfully reflected in these sonnets, sometimes in exquisite bits of verse.

The power of observation which they show, however, is by no means of a close, informative kind, but rather of the large, vague, impression-gathering order. There is much less piquancy or novelty of detail than we might expect. Here and there we have a plain yet tender line like

A barn by many seasons beaten gray.

But very seldom does the poet delight us by raising a homely feature into poetic significance. It is not too much to say that these sonnets, with all their brilliant impressionism, hardly enrich our sense of Canadian rural life with more than some fine scenic images. This narrow range of observational power is evident in the absence of any direct treatment of human life, of human as distinguished from naturalistic sentiment, and helps to deprive this sonnet series of popular and realistic elements. In the sonnet *Mowing*, for example, there are fine bits of impressionism:

This is the voice of high midsummer's heat.
The rasping, vibrant clamour soars and shrills.

The "crying knives" are noticed at their work, the "fate that smote" the clover and the timothy tops is mentioned, and the sestet takes a flight to describe the action of the sun which "with chemic ray seals up each cordial essence in its cell," and thus imprisons the "spirit of June" to cheer the cattle some winter's day "in their dusky stalls." But there is no mention of mowers; there is no human figure in the field. This artistic asceticism may be serviceable in obtaining a certain purity of impressionistic effect, as it is in the landscapes of some of the Barbizon school of painters. But for poetry at least the example of Millet is probably better than that of Rousseau, as Roberts himself has proved. At any rate this is almost sufficient of itself to make a severance between Roberts and the public of our time, which seems to demand a vigorous presentation of life as the first condition of its listening to any ideal or imaginative strain the poet may have to sing to it.

Nor is the poetry of these sonnets likely to make any strong appeal to a more philosophically minded class of readers, that class which ultimately came to the support of Wordsworth and his austerely contemplative Muse. The sonnet sequence hardly leaves any strong unity of moral impression on our minds. There is a want of basal note in Roberts in this respect which makes his poetry little more than a wavering impression taken from the surface of things and giving no comfort, no stay to the mind. The moralisings which the poet occasionally intro-duces into the sestet are either commonplace or very fanciful,

26

or easily recognised as the well-known vein of some great poet. The moral appended to *The Cow Pasture* is Browning's recognition of imperfection as a stimulus; that of *Where the Cattle Come to Drink* is Wordsworth's oft-preached "dignity of common toil;" those of *The Cicada in the Firs, The Oat-Threshing* and *The Autumn Thistles* are coldly or cheaply wrought fantasies. But Mr. Roberts is weakest in the altitudes of meditative thought, as in *The Stillness of the Frost*. "Such," he says, after describing the "frost-white wood" and "the ineffable pallor" of the blue sky—

Such, I must think, even at the dawn of Time
Was thy white hush, O world, when thou lay'st cold,
Unwaked to love, new from the Maker's word,
And the spheres, watching, stilled their high accord
To marvel at perfection in thy mould,
The grace of thine austerity sublime!

That is Robert Pollok come again and the forgotten sublimities of *The Course of Time*.

With all his gifts, then, Roberts evidently lacks two things without which a poet in our day cannot take a strong hold of the public. He does not as a poet give us either a lively, vigorous presentation of life or a profound and critical interpretation of it.

Roberts' poetry, one may see, remains very much a pure literary tradition, the element of natural impulse in it being hardly strong enough to make original moulds for itself. His diction, in particular, owes much to literary tradition; it is that of a school, the school of impressionistic description which arose as the aftermath of the poetry of Keats and Tennyson. It is true he shows quite remarkable power and facility in its use. Even when he approaches too perceptibly to the mould of Keats or Tennyson, it is in the manner of one who has learned to see and feel with the master rather than merely to imitate his style.

This is a wonder-cup in Summer's hand.
    Sombre, impenetrable round its rim
    The fir-trees bend and brood. The noons o'erbrim
The windless hollow of its iris'd strand
With mote-thick sun and water-breathings bland.

That is from the *Summer Pool*, and shows how cleverly Roberts has made his own the luxuriance and iridescence of the master's style. But the master's art is always something of a dangerous legacy to the school, and the general result, especially when the biting verb of Swinburne and some refinements of Rossetti are added to the Keatsian assortment, has been to establish a kind of poetic diction which has at length become just as conventional as that old diction of the eighteenth century which Wordsworth drove from the field. The defects of this school are, in general, an over-fullness and indiscriminate intensity of language and a love of euphuistic novelties, which are now ceasing to be novel and are hardening into an artificial poetic vocabulary. How often the same tricksy word serves to make the effect:

A yellow hillside *washed* in airy seas
Of azure,

Amber wastes of sky

Washing the ridge.
How the harsh stalks are *washed* with radiance new.

In this style every trait is pressed to the utmost. The "murmuring streams" and "vocal reeds" of the 18th century school have given place to the "long-drawn sobbings of the reed-choked surge;" waves or waters no longer wash the shore, they "pulse;" the dawn no longer chills, it "bites;" it does not rise, it "leaps;" it is nothing so common as rosy, it may be "white," however, but it has more frequently some elusive epithet attached to it, such as "inviolate" or "incommunicable," or "liturgical." We no longer seek or search, we "quest." Darkness and night "reel," the sea almost always "sobs" now, the wind, the trees, the rain, all "sob," though "grieve" may be admitted as a variety; the sky is preferably "sapphirine" now as regards colour, and "inviolable" in ethical suggestion. The silence of the stars or the stillness of the woods is pretty sure to require the use of "expectant" or "expectancy" for its interpretation. Certain terms are great favourites, and are called on for hard work of a kind they were not always accustomed to, as for example, "largess," "lure," "elemental," "assuaged and unassuaged," "sinister," "bourgeoned," "tranced," "bland," "winnowing," "throb" and "kiss" are common drudges in the school. Privative forms have risen into great demand, the hills are "unbowed," abysses "unsunned," probably without any thought of Euripides, eyelids "unlifting;" in two members of the school I noted "unremembrance." All the great poets of the past, of course, may contribute something to this impressionistic vocabulary. Shakespeare

28

once made the seas "multitudinous," now the voices of night, the silences of the forest, the hum of thoroughfares and all similar phenomena are frequently "multitudinous;" we even get from one poet "the multitudinous friendliness of the sea," which is probably not without thought of Æschylus. Wordsworth once made a striking use of "incommunicable," now a slightly more elusive use of it in connection with "light" or "space" or "rhyme" or "word" meets us at every turn. A fine discovery which catches the fancy of the school soon obtains its hall-mark. In Henley the river is "new-mailed" in the morning light, in Roberts the ice-bound pools are in "diamond mail," in Wilfred Campbell the river is "sun-cuirassed."

All this, of course, is but the natural history of style, the evolution of a new poetic diction which has arisen to meet the needs of modern poetry with its more intimate sense of the mystery of life and nature. But it is evidently beginning to harden in its mould, and the modern poet will have to beware of it. It has become the mark of a half-affected intensity of sentiment and the expression of an imaginative insight which is only derivative and superficial.

V.—THE *AVE*. REFLECTIVE POETRY, THE BOOK OF THE NATIVE

IN 1892 Mr. Roberts published the *Ave*, a poem for the centenary of Shelley. In this poem he once more makes use of a grand traditional form of poetry, for the *Ave* belongs both by its elevation of style and its manner of treating the subject to that high imaginative form of elegy which Shelley's *Adonais*, Arnold's *Thyrsis* and Swinburne's *Ave atque Vale* have made familiar to English readers.

A sea this is—beware who ventureth!
For like a fiord the narrow floor is laid
Mid-ocean deep to the sheer mountain walls.

These lines, which Mr. R.W. Gilder wrote of the sonnet, might be applied with even more truth to this high form of elegy. There is no poetry which needs a more mystic, intimate and profoundly essential contact with its subject than this elegiac chant of the poet over his dead brother. It must be, in order to hold its place in that great line of tradition which reaches from the first idyll of Theocritus to the *Ave atque Vale*, a subtle and strangely perfect expression of the spirit and genius of the departed one. It is the modern poet's visit to the nether world of shades, in which

Piping a ditty sad for Bion's fate,

30

he seeks the soul of his lost brother in the immortal gloom, and gives the world something like a farewell vision of him. And the worth of the vision lies not merely in the high, impassioned music of the song, but in the way in which the lost Bion's figure assumes the transcendent and almost impersonal outlines of an elemental spiritual force that has been withdrawn from the sum of life. In such work there is no room for the commoner style of characterisation and estimate which may fitly find a place in ordinary eulogistic and memorial verse. The strain is altogether of a higher mood, and the logic scorns the ordinary limits of thought, to use a mystic symbolism of its own. You may, if you like, use all the remote and unreal conventions which have distinguished pastoral elegy since its birth, but you must give them an atmosphere, a far depth of outlook over human fate and history, in which they become again, for once, all true. You may call upon Pan and the Nymphs with Theocritus, or upon the "mighty mother" with Shelley, or like Swinburne have visions of the "gods of gloom" and

That thing transformed which was the Cytherean.

But all these things must be felt as a sincere symbolism of a mystery in which the fate of the poet living and that of his dead brother are alike bound or even blended. There is immense license for the imagination, yet nowhere is the call for sincerity in the deepest sense of the word more imperative.

In the *Adonais*, for example, the thought sweeps wildly through that vast, vague, pantheistic and Platonic universe in which Shelley's soul dwelt, but there is a transcendental harmony and unity in the assemblage of elements there, contradictory and incongruous as they might seem in the work of another. That is Shelley's world, from which his cry comes to us with a passionate sincerity:

Dust to the dust, but the pure spirit shall flow
　　Back to the burning fountain whence it came,
A portion of the Eternal, which must glow
　　Through time and change unquenchably the same,
Whilst thy cold embers choke the sordid hearth of shame.
Peace, peace! he is not dead, he doth not sleep!
　　He hath awakened from the dream of life;
'Tis we who, lost in stormy visions, keep
　　With phantoms an unprofitable strife.

So in the *Ave atque Vale*, Swinburne's impassioned elegy for Baudelaire, all the strange forms of imaginative appeal from the "god of suns and songs" to the "god bitter and luxurious," are true formulas for the psychic life alike of the singer and of him who is the subject of the song. And the lyrical cry is in full accord with the feeling of the whole:

Not thee, O never thee, in all time's changes,
Not thee, but this the sound of thy sad soul.

This form of elegy, indeed, may be said to require for its happiest accomplishment a strong moral and even mental affinity to exist between the singer and his lost brother, otherwise the song lacking confidence and intimacy would fail somewhere of its effect.

Mr. Roberts calls his poem an ode, but, on the whole, he makes it conform to the requirements of the pastoral elegy. He begins by some stanzas which describe the scenery of his own Tantramar and the high intimations and visitations which came to him there. In this way, rather than by any more intimate and psychological method, he modestly ventures to associate his own psychic and poetic world with that of the poet of the *Prometheus*. The manner, however, in which he makes the transition from the one theme to the other is forced and unnatural. After describing the ebb and flow of the tides in the marshes of Tantramar, he continues thus:

Strangely akin you seem to him whose birth
One hundred years ago,
With fiery succour to the ranks of song
Defied the ancient gates of wrath and wrong.

That is a disenchanting glimpse of the artist's hand in a moment of embarrassment and difficulty, and quite destroys the impression of inevitableness which poetry should give.

After eleven stanzas devoted to Tantramar the poet begins a series of lofty characterisations of the genius of Shelley as exhibited in his principal poems. There is an imaginative brilliancy about these characterisations. They are large, loose and sweeping, but for that very reason they are particularly suited to the nature of the subject. Indeed, the large, rhetorical fluency of the style has something which in its way resembles the wide sweep and movement of Shelley's own glance. The following stanzas are a fair example of the very mingled yarn of fine and commonplace in the *Ave*:

The star that burns on revolution smote
    Wild heats and change on thine ascendant sphere,

Whose influence thereafter seemed to float
   Through many a strange eclipse of wrath and fear,
Dimming awhile the radiance of thy love.
   But still supreme in thy nativity,
All dark, invidious aspects far above,
   Beamed one clear orb for thee—
The star whose ministrations just and strong
Controlled the tireless flight of Dante's song.

With how august contrition, and what tears
   Of penitential, unavailing shame,
Thy venerable foster-mother hears
   The sons of song impeach her ancient name,
Because in one rash hour of anger blind
   She thrust thee forth in exile, and thy feet
Too soon to earth's wild outer ways consigned—
   Far from her well-loved seat,
Far from her studious halls and storied towers
And weedy Isis winding through his flowers.

And thou, thenceforth the breathless child of change,
   Thine own Alastor, on in endless quest
Of unimagined loveliness didst range,
   Urged ever by the soul's divine unrest.
Of that high quest and that unrest divine
   Thy first immortal music thou didst make,
Inwrought with fairy Alp, and Reuss, and Rhine,
   And phantom seas that break
In soundless foam along the shores of Time,
Prisoned in thine imperishable rhyme.

I would not like to have to mark all the common and
coarsely hazarded phrases in the *Ave*, but still there is a fervour
and intensity of utterance in it which redeems its faults in this
way and gives it as a whole the excellence of spontaneity and
vigour. At times, too, particularly where the poet has the direct
support of imaginative associations from Shelley's own writings, the *Ave* has a fine and rare quality of imaginative characterisation, as in the apostrophe to the Baths of Caracalla and
that sky of Rome from which Shelley, as he tells us himself,
drew a subtle strength and inspiration while writing his
Prometheus Unbound:

O Baths of Caracalla, arches clad
   In such transcendent rhapsodies of green,
That one might guess the sprites of spring were glad

For your majestic ruin, yours the scene,
The illuminating air of sense and thought;
    And yours the enchanted light, O skies of Rome,
Where the great vision into form was wrought;

Beneath your blazing dome

The intensest song our language ever knew
Beat up exhaustless to the blinding blue!

In the last part of the poem, from the twenty-first stanza onwards, the *Ave* begins to assume the character of grand elegiac vision and lament; the poet ventures on freer wing into the high, ethereal region into which the *Lycidas* and the *Adonais* followed their Greek models, and we hear again all the well-known elegiac cries:

Mourn, Mediterranean waters, mourn
    In affluent purple down your golden shores!

or,

Not thou, not thou—for thou wert in the light
    Of the Unspeakable, where time is not.

The general treatment in this part resembles most that of the *Adonais*. There is a free mingling of tones and fancies from every region of thought, the orthodox Christian hope, the conception of an "eventual element of calm," as Browning's *Cleon* describes it, and the classical Elysian vision, Homer, Plato, Job, Omar, Shakespeare and the rest of the immortals greeting the latest comer.

There face to face thou sawest the living God
    And worshippedst, beholding Him the same
Adored on earth as Love .   .   .   .   .   .
    .   .   .   .
    In that unroutable profound of peace,
Beyond experience of pulse and breath,
    Beyond the last release
Of longing, rose to greet thee all the lords
Of Thought, with consummation in their words:
He of the seven cities claimed, whose eyes
    Though blind, saw gods and heroes, and the fall
Of Ilium, and many alien skies
    And Circe's isle; and he etc., etc,

The poet even uses the great freedom of vision allowed in this species of poem to describe Shelley's disembodied spirit looking on at his own obsequies:

> And thou didst contemplate with wonder strange
> And curious regard thy kindred flame
> Fed sweet with frankincense and wine and salt,
> With fierce purgation search thee. . . .

In the ecstatic flow of images and utterance which characterises this last part of the poem there is a wonderful mixture of the true and the false, the beautiful and the commonplace, the grand and the grandiose. The *Ave* is a splendid rhetorical effort, a bold but somewhat unregulated flight of fancy through the empyrean, marked by many irrelevancies, of course, and mistaken toyings with every breeze that blows. It gives us some very fine characterisations of Shelley's genius, but it can hardly be said to create a new elegiac world for us or add a new and pure mould to the great elegies of the past. It owes something to the vigorous flow of its verse. The great 10-line stanza with the strong cadence of its closing couplet, made stronger by the shortening of the preceding line, is urged, through modulations and harmonies not always of the finest or smoothest kind, into great vigour of movement; and sometimes, as in the 18th, 23rd and 24th stanzas, reaches high melodic effects. In the *Ave*, as elsewhere, the work of Roberts has nothing either of the weakness or fineness of inlay work; its qualities are rather those of the improvisatore.

All the poems of Roberts which we have passed in review so far, belong more or less to the poetry of nature description, unless the *Ave* be a partial exception. But during the last decade of the nineteenth century the poet had evidently begun to feel that he had done his best in that region and might now try something a little different. At any rate in his next volume, *The Book of the Native*, published in 1897, most of the poems have a new critical and reflective vein in them. It is a very mixed vein, as the character of Roberts' thought in poetry always is, drawing from different and heterogeneous sources with a kind of inconscient recklessness. The *Heal-All*, for example, is a pure Wordsworthian product in phrase, ethical feeling and reflection:

> Thy unobtrusive purple face
> Amid the meagre grass

Greets me with long remembered grace,
    And cheers me as I pass.   .   .   .   .   .

.   .   .   .

Thy simple wisdom I would gain,—
To heal the hurt Life brings,
With kindly cheer, and faith in pain,
    And joy of common things.

The *Quest of the Arbutus*, on the other hand, is pure
Emersonian optimism with touches of Emersonian phrase:

Because the tardy gods grew kind,
Unrest and care were cast behind;
I took a day and found the world
Was fashioned to my mind.

But it ends suddenly on the chord of the sentimental:

And then the world's expectancy
Grew clear: I knew its need to be
Not this dear flower, but one dear hand
To pluck the flower with me.

That last is a note which has not been much heard in
Roberts' poetry as yet, but is soon to rise much higher and
almost silence all the others. But not yet. At this time the most
striking feature of his poetry is a kind of philosophic mysticism, which might be considered as one way of escaping from
the traditional point of view which had grown banal for poetry
by much repetition. For the poetry of Roberts at this period,
like Canadian poetry in general, still held by the old ethical
traditions of the great English and American schools of the
previous generation. It was virtually unstirred by the subtle
reactions of thought, the love of ethical paradox and the
neurotic delicacy of sensibility which characterise the French
Verlaines and Mallarmés of the time. Not a ripple from the
Chat Noir and the cafés by the Seine had touched it, as the
verse of Bliss Carman, for example, had already been touched
by the manner and sentiment of the *Romances Sans Paroles*.
It was in the direction of a philosophic mysticism, then, for
which Emerson had already in a measure prepared the American public, that Roberts now sought an escape from the ordinary, from the traditional, from the grand ethical highway of
the poets now become too much of a common thoroughfare.
The form which this philosophic mysticism takes in such

poems as *Autochthon* and *The Unsleeping* may be described as a poetic treatment of the cosmic process, and owes a good deal to Emerson, whose curt and keen-edged phrase set the style for this oracular verse. Here are some lines from *Autochthon*:

I am the spirit astir
    To swell the grain
When fruitful suns confer
    With labouring rain;
I am the life that thrills
    In branch and bloom;
I am the patience of abiding hills,
    The promise masked in doom.

   .   .   .   .   .

I am the hush of calm,
    I am the speed,
The flood-tide's triumphant psalm,
    The marsh pool's heed;
I work in rocking roar
    Where cataracts fall;
I flash in the prismy fire that dances o'er
    The dew's ephemeral ball.

The Unsleeping is in the same. style of thought, only in a different metre:

I heave aloft the smoking hill:
To silent peace its throes I still,
But ever at its heart of fire
I lurk, an unassuaged desire.
I wrap me in the sightless germ
An instant or an endless term;
And still its atoms are my care,
Dispersed in ashes or in air.

Modern science has taken much of the mysticism out of this old Emersonian vein. The idea of one power which works through all things has been made so definite by the far-reaching monistic conceptions of modern science that it is a very easy task for any poet to personify it and illustrate it throughout the whole length and breadth of natural phenomena in the universe. It is a cosmic process which explains all and engulfs all in a principle of absolute identity. It includes everything without adding a definite idea to anything. Professor Rand, I notice, is quite as nimble in making use of it as Mr. Roberts

37

is. His poem "I Am" has just as good a right to the title of "Autochthon" or "The Unsleeping" as these have to the title of "I Am."

I am in blush of the rose,
  The shimmer of dawn;
Am girdle Orion knows,
  The fount undrawn.

I am earth's potency,
  The chemic ray, the rain's,
The reciprocity
  That loads the wains.

In *Origins* the treatment is different. The cosmic process now appears as scientifically impersonal and involving the human race in the material chain of phenomena:

Inexorably decreed
By the ancestral deed,
The puppets of our sires,
We work out blind desires,
And for our sons ordain
The blessing or the bane.
In ignorance we stand
With fate in either hand,
And question stars and earth

Of life, and death, and birth,
With wonder in our eyes
We scan the kindred skies,
While through the common grass
Our atoms mix and pass.

At the end of the poem, however, Mr. Roberts rescues himself from the grasp of this sombre scientific necessitarianism in a manner which the professors of metaphysics will regard, I fear, as another instance of poetic levity:

But in the urge intense
And fellowship of sense,
Suddenly comes a word
In other ages heard.
On a great wind our souls
Are borne to unknown goals,
And past the bournes of space
To the unaverted Face.

This sudden leap of faith as an immediate antithesis to admitted scientific fact is hardly as happy as Browning's famous use of it against philosophic doubt:

Just when we are safest, there is a sunset touch, etc.

Faith does not make a good antithesis to scientific fact; but yet, taking it in a large view, it is true that the word "in other ages heard" is the centre of that impulse which will not wholly yield the ground to science.

But, as a matter of fact, this logical opposition of diverging lines of thought gives the poet no trouble. In *Ascription, Immanence, Earth's Complines* and other poems of this collection, it disappears completely, and the cosmic process presents itself with equal facility as under the direct control of the Creator:

O Thou who hast beneath Thy hand
The dark foundations of the land,
The motion of whose ordered thought
An instant universe hath wrought.

Who hast within they equal heed
The rolling sun, the ripening seed,
The azure of the speedwell's eye
The vast solemnities of sky.

Who hear'st no less the feeble note
Of one small bird's awakening throat,
Than that unnamed, tremendous chord
Arcturus sounds before his Lord.

Every age has its own language. *Ascription* is a fine new 19th century dress for Addison's Ode. Instead of "the spacious firmament on high" read "the vast sublimities of sky," and for the "spangled heavens proclaim," etc., read "that unnamed tremendous chord" which Arcturus sounds.

These philosophical poems are an interesting reflection of the general attitude of our age in matters of faith and knowledge. The easy way in which it holds in its mind diverging theories and lines of thought without caring to pursue them to the point at which contradictions make themselves harshly felt, accepting each to some extent as having its truth, bridging over difficulties with a hazy logic, and waiting without much anxiety for a solution which will preserve all it wants to preserve, this attitude, very characteristic of the Anglo-Saxon mind in particular, has much practical wisdom in it. But one would not consider the poetry which reflects this attitude so naively to be much of a contribution to the interpretation of life. There are some sweet, natural notes, however, in *The Book of the Native* when the poet lays aside philosophic theory, which is generally a poor support for poetic fancy, and gives a free expression to what he feels, to what he hopes or fears, as in this, from *Kinship:*

> Back to wisdom take me, mother,
>   Comfort me with kindred hands;
> Teach me tales the world's forgetting
>   Till my spirit understands.
>
> Tell me how some sightless impulse,
>   Working out a hidden plan,
> God for kin and clay for fellow,
>   Wakes to find itself a man.

Or this from *Recessional:*

> Moth and blossom, blade and bee,
> Worlds must go as well as we,
>   In the long procession joining
> Mount and star, and sea.
>
> Toward the shadowy brink we climb
> Where the round year rolls sublime;
>   Rolls, and drops, and falls forever
> In the vast of time;
>
> Like a plummet plunging deep
> Past the utmost reach of sleep,
>   Till remembrance has no longer
> Care to laugh or weep.

That is the old lyrical note of Longfellow, a little amplified by modern phrase, but still simple and tender, and it seems to be the note most natural to Roberts in those reflective poems.

VI.—POETRY OF THE CITY. NEW YORK NOCTURNES. EROTIC POEMS. THE ROSE OF LIFE. CONCLUSION

IN 1896, or thereabouts, Mr. Roberts resigned his Professor's chair at King's College, Nova Scotia, and went to New York to push his literary career there. Years before, indeed, in one of his poems, "The Poet Bidden to Manhattan Island," he had hinted he might have to leave a country which was too poor to pay its authors, at least its poets, suitably:

> You've piped at home, where none could pay,
>   Til now, I trust, your wits are riper.
> Make no delay, but come this way,
>   And pipe for them that pay the piper!

Possibly the reasons for the migration of our Canadian poet lay deeper. In a more tranquil age he might have been content to go on writing Canadian lyrics and idylls and drawing the modest academic salary; and who knows but some day that ardent, aspiring genius of his which has tried so many forms might at last have found a supreme one and produced an immortal song? But the fever of the time has got into the blood of our literary men. The immense, cheap successes of the popular novel and play and the opulence of the successful journalist in the great cities have unsettled them. They seek the support of professional circles and syndicates, of patriotic associations and popular fashions; above all, they seek the support of an atmosphere which has a certain stimulating effect on their faculties, mainly in the direction, I think, of forcing a more rapid adjustment of their powers to the calls of the day and the hour. Spenser might write his great ideal song in the Irish wilds of Kilcolman, but our characteristic modern works with their near actuality of theme, the poetry of Henley, the comedies and literary criticism of Howells, the stories of Harding, come from men who breathe the atmosphere of our great cities. Their writings reflect the quickly passing spirit of the time, often of the hour, in which they live, and their material is of a raw kind, hard to transform into the highest moulds of art, because it consists of types and a social environment which they can hardly yet feel, any more than Jane Austen did in her novels, in their full and pathetic significance. Even Thackeray's strongest figures, his Colonel Newcomes and Rawdon Crawleys and his wonderful journalists, were reminiscences with a soft shading of the past about them, rather than mere transcripts of the passing day. But that is by the way, though it is not without its bearing on the new "poetry of the city" which Mr. Arthur Symons declares is the true form of poetry "which professes to be modern."

Mr. Roberts did not use to have so high an opinion of the "heedless throngs and traffic of cities" as he describes them in one of his poems, but like every one else he feels the set of the tide in these days. Accordingly his *New York Nocturnes*, the latest of the collections in this one volume edition, is a contribution to this "poetry of the city."

The romance of New York at night, the nocturnal brilliancy of its lighted pavements, the endless tide of movement, the fascinating privacy of its crowds, Mr. Roberts has come to think that there is poetry there as well as in the vale of Tempe and Canadian forest clearings. So there is, though the characteristic quality and aroma of it may be another matter. He does not, however, attempt to treat the subject with the breadth and boldness of Mr. Henley's *London Voluntaries*, where the English poet struggles hard to render in the freest and most adaptable form of verse the elemental vigour and movement of city life,

> This insolent and comely stream
> Of appetence, this freshet of desire.

Mr. Roberts does, however, give us some vivid impressionistic pictures of city phenomena at night:

Above the vanishing faces
    A phantom train fares on
With a voice that shakes the shadows,—
    Diminishes, and is gone.

But there is less of this kind of work in the *New York Nocturnes* than one might have expected from a hand so deft with the impressionistic brush in other regions. The fact is, that in these poems the poet has begun to gravitate in another direction, towards the sentimental and erotic poetry of the Rosetti school. That is the form in which he now seeks to escape from the moral commonplace which holds us all in its clutches. The roar of Broadway at night, the thunder of the elevated railway and the glare of light at the railway station, are but the environment of "Me and Thee," of a passion that expresses itself with all the warm abandonment of the poet of the Religion of Beauty:

The street is full of lights and cries,
    The crowd but brings thee close to me.
I only hear thy low replies;
    I only see thine eyes.

That is an epitome of the *New York Nocturnes*. It is a new Laura, whose phantom-like existence in the background of these poems is the artistic support for the poet's fancy, a Laura not enshrined as once by the running streams and woods, and the *aer sacro sereno* of Valclusa, but met amidst the hurrying throngs of Sixth Avenue or trysting at the New York Central Station.

The poetry of *New York Nocturnes* marks the beginning of a change in Mr. Roberts which amounts almost to an entire transformation of his literary or poetic ideals. One whole phase of his poetic career has come to an end, and he is to live, at any rate he is to write, less under those old influences which emanated from Rydal Mount and Concord and other sacred seats of the Muses, and more under those of our new literary, democratic Bohemia represented by poets like Mr. Henley, who sings of London crowds, and has transferred Pan from Mount Maenalus to Piccadilly. The poetry of *Actaeon* and the *Sonnet Sequence* and *The Book of the Native* belonged essentially in its spirit and its form to the great orthodox traditional schools of the nineteenth century. It had all the reverence and decorum of priestly and prophetic utterance, it was full of chaste reticence and high conventions. The new poetry of the

43

Nocturnes and *The Rose of Life* is the poetry of an age which
is filled with the desire of life and eager to gratify every sense,
an age which has given up the pale doctrine of self-suppres-
sion. It was only the other day Mr. Swinburne was singing its
song of triumph in *Harper's Monthly*, and congratulating it on
having escaped from the shadow of that dread God of the
Hebrews:

> The dark old God who had slain him grew on with the
> Christ he slew,
> And poison was rank in the grain that with growth of his
> Gospel grew.
> And the blackness of darkness brightened, and red in the
> heart of the flame,
> Shone down as a blessing that lightened, the curse of a new
> God's name,
> Through centuries of burning and trembling belief as a
> signal it shone
> Till man, soul sick of dissembling, bade fear and her frauds
> begone.

> . . . .

> The song of the day of thy fury when nature and death
> shall quail,
> Rings now as the thunders of Jewry, the ghost of a dead
> world's tale.

That way of looking at the history of mankind, through the
blood-shot eyes of a Maenad, one might say, is surely not a
very wise one. If the white man's civilisation means anything
we can be proud of, it means that he has not only kept clear
of deifying the orgiastic instinct in human nature, but that on
the whole he has not imposed greater restrictions on his life
than were good for him at that time, or used stronger sanctions
than were necessary to enforce them. So far as he tended in
the past to raise altars either to Moloch or to the Pandemian
Venus, it was the worship of the "dark old God of the
Hebrews" mainly that suppressed the tendency. The tempo-
rary tyranny of sects and hierarchies has little to do with the
fundamental aspects of the matter. You cannot read man's
history profitably as that of a nigger escaped from the lash, nor
celebrate it wisely with Phrygian timbrels; no, not even if you
have the ear of an Apollo for lyrical medody.

Naturally one of the notes to make itself more clearly heard
in the new poetry is the erotic one which Rossetti, then singing
in the colder atmosphere of another generation, introduced, in

a delicate, mystic Dantean form, into English poetry. This is the dominant note in Roberts' latest volume, *The Rose of Life*. The erotic poetry of that volume has something of the delicate reserve which characterises the vein of Rossetti, and it combines, in much of the same way as he does, aesthetic self-abandonment with the mystic idealism of the *Vita Nuova*. To look on the beloved one is to understand the secret of the universe, "the meaning of all things that are."* Mr. Roberts makes use of this sentiment with characteristic vigour:

> The world becomes a little thing;
> Art, travel, music, men
> And all that these can ever give
> Are in her brow's white ken.

Sometimes, indeed, he uses it with more vigour than delicacy:

> How little I knew, when I first saw you,
> And your eyes for a moment questioned mine,
> It amounted to this—that the dawn and the dew,
> The midnight's dark and the midmoon's shine,
> The awe of the silent, soaring peak,
> The harebell's hue and the cloud in the blue,
> And all the beauty I sing and seek,
> Would come to mean—just you!

There is something of the recklessness of the *improvisatore* in that assembly of images.

This mystical element, however, which comes all the way from Dante and the Italian sonneteers of the 14th century, is frequently steeped by the modern poet in a warmer atmosphere of sense-impression than was the custom with the poet of the *Vita Nuova* at least. Roberts' *Attar* has the full red of the erotic chord:

> The pulses of your throat
>   What madness they denote to me,—
> Passion, and hunger, and despair,
>   And ecstacy and prayer to me!
>
> The dark bloom of your flesh
>   Is as a magic mesh to me,
> Wherein our spirits lie ensnared,
>   Your wild, wild beauty bared to me.

Indeed, there is the same ethical variety or heterogeneity in

Roberts' new erotic vein as there is in his other poetry. In the poem which gives its title to this volume, *The Rose of Life*, the sentiment has the peculiar bitter savour which you find in Beaudelaire or Swinburne.

The Rose asks "Why am I sad?" that is, what is the meaning of this infinite sadness and subtlety in Desire? And a Wind, "older than Time" and "wiser than Sleep," replies:

The cries of a thousand lovers,
A thousand slain,
The tears of all the forgotten
Who kissed in vain,
And the journeying years that have vanished
Have left on you
The witness, each, of its pain,
Ancient, yet new.
So many lives you have lived;
So many a star
Hath veered in the signs to make you
The wonder you are!
And this is the price of your beauty:
Your wild soul is thronged
With the phantoms of joy unfulfilled
That beauty hath wronged,
With the pangs of all secret betrayals,
The ghosts of desire,
The bite of old flame, and the chill
Of the ashes of fire.

Something of the livid vein of Beaudelaire has begun to tinge the bright red of Rossetti there. There is a perceptible odour of those poison-flowers of the French poet which bloom only in charnel-houses and have the scent of death about them. The poem would read impressively as a characterisation of some type of beauty like Swinburne's *Faustine*. There is a kinship in the thought of the two poems as well as in certain subtleties of style and rhythm:

For in the time we know not of
    Did fate begin
Weaving the web of days that wove
    Your doom, Faustine?

The poetry of Roberts' last volume seems to take us a long way from the poet of "The Songs of the Common Day" and "The Book of the Native," with their sober Wordsworthian tones and pious sublimities. But we need not mistake. It is only a canter which Roberts, the artist, is taking into that region of

Fierce loves and lovely leaf-buds poisonous.

No doubt, the change of note denotes some change of intellectual centre in the artist's life and some liberation of sentiment due to a change in his circumstances. But the very variety of ethical tone in Roberts shows how much poetry is to him a matter of art, rather than the deep, essential distillation of his life, the concentrated essence of it from which everything secondary and derivative is excluded as valueless. The title of one of his volumes, "In Divers Tones," might be written over them all. The moral impulse toward song which is so pure and unisonant in the poetry of a Longfellow and a Wordsworth, for example, and for that matter in a Rossetti and Beaudelaire also, is capable of assuming any shape in Roberts with the greatest facility. Sometimes it is a Wordsworthian moral that inspires him as in the sonnet, *Where the Cattle Come to Drink*:

A lesson of the calm of humble creed,
The simple dignity of common toil
And the plain wisdom of unspoken prayer.

Sometimes it is the call of Tennysonian lyrical sentiment and melody:

Oh, clear in the sphere of the air,   Clear, clear, tender
and far.

Sometimes it is the blood-red glare of Swinburne's vision and his fiercely urged phrase, as in *Khartoum*:

Set in the fierce red desert for a sword
Drawn and deep-driven implacably! The tide
Of scorching sand that chafes thy landward side
Storming they palms.

Sometimes it is Rossetti's imaginative self-abandonment to dream and desire, as in *A Nocturne of Trysting*:

And life and hope and joy seem but a faint prevision
Of the flower that is thy body and the flame that is thy soul.

Or it is the solemn, religious strain of *Ascription*:

O thou who hast beneath thy hand.

Or it is a note from Browning, or it is still surviving in his muse, the languor of Keatsian reverie. In this very volume of

The Rose of Life, filled as it is with subtle perfumes from the poetry of Rossetti and Swinburne, there is also a capital imitation of Kipling's manner in the poem called *The Stranded Ship*, which has all the swing of that master's verse and his healthy feeling for the romance of modern adventure:

No more she mounts the circles from Fundy to the Horn.
From Cuba to the Cape runs down the tropic morn,
Explores the Vast Uncharted where great bergs ride in
    ranks,
Nor shouts a broad "Ahoy" to the dories on the Banks.

But that a poet could, even from the point of view of mere art, write poems of such diversity of tone, is a striking illustration of the curious breadth and complexity of the spirit of our time. It is the old story of the Renaissance over again, with its desire to lay hold of every side of life, and that mixture of sentiment which Browning has satirised in the Bishop of St. Praxed's:

That bas-relief in bronze ye promised me,
Those Pans and Nymphs ye wot of, and perchance
Some tripod, thyrsus, and a vase or so,
The Saviour at his sermon on the Mount,
Saint Praxed in a glory, and one Pan
Ready to twitch the Nymph's last garment off,
And Moses with the tables.

But our more self-conscious age cannot attain to such breadth without feeling the moral contrarieties there are to dispose of.

There are samples, also, of our old friend, the cosmic process in poetry, in this volume, and a psychological poem *On the Upper Deck*, which leaves a somewhat faint impression on the mind as of a Gibson young man and woman playing at poetry and Browning. Some light lyrics in Part II are amongst the best things in the book. *Shepherdess Fair*, for example, covers a fine gravity and truth of feeling under a light play of fancy:

O shepherdess brown, O shepherdess fair,
Where are my flocks you have in care?
My wonderful, white, wide-pasturing sheep
Of dream and desire and tears and sleep,
Many the flocks, but small the care
You give to their keeping, O shepherdess fair!

O shepherdess gay, your flocks have fed
By the iris pool, by the saffron bed,
Till now by noon they have wandered far,
And you have forgotten where they are!

O shepherdess fair, O shepherdess wild,
Full wise are your flocks, but you a child!

You shall not be chid if you let them stray
In your own wild way, in your own child way,
You will call them all back at the close of day.

Large brain and soul, and many-hued web of thought, dream and desire, all in the keeping of sweet and twenty, who is distractingly naive—a fancy worthy of Heine, and set to words which have something of his charm without his bitterness.

As one may see from that last poem, Roberts has a true gift for lyrical verse. Nothing he writes in that way is ever wanting in vigour and natural freedom of movement. He has not the same command of the high and more sedate harmonies of blank verse. That is a great and treacherously smooth sea in which, if he does not quite sink, he soon begins to show a jaded and mechanical action. Monotony, unmeaning emphasis, solemnly factitious pauses, forced rushes of melody, cadences abruptly quenched in the sand-flats of the next line, these are the penalties for him who ventures over-boldly. But in lyrical measures, and especially in light movements, Roberts' verse has admirable qualities, truth of accent, spontaneity and vigour of movement, the nobler elements in metrical art. He has nothing of the smooth and subtle workmanship which is the pride of the modern aesthetic school. He may at times have a Tennysonian smoothness of effect but it is not a native quality of his verse. It is noticeable, however, that in his last volume the moulds of his verse are fresher and more modern than the old ones which he learned in the school of Tennyson and Longfellow. There is more freedom in the new metrical moulds and a cunning use of iterations and disguised refrains which in such clever hands gives an ear-haunting quality to the verse.

On the whole this new volume shows a certain novelty of tone and treatment and a tendency to introduce more rounded and concrete shapes of life into his poetry which may have considerable significance for the poet's future. Penhaps our best Canadian poets have devoted themselves too much to an almost abstract form of nature poetry which has too little savour of the national life and the national sentiment about it and is more dependent on literary tradition than they seem to be aware of. Mr. Drummond with his Habitant idylls is of course a notable exception, and the success they have met with shows what a ready public after all there always is for a true and lively presentation of life. It may be said that the vehicle which he uses, the broken English of Jean Baptiste, can hardly be considered a classical form for the expression of French-Canadian character:

Yes—yes—Pelang, mon cher garçon!
    I t'ink of you. t'ink of you, night an' day,
Don't mak' no difference seems to me
    How long de tam you was gone away.

After all it is hard for a French-Canadian to get over the fact that the language in which Marie really thinks of her Pelang is not that but something nearer the sweet note of *La Claire Fontaine*. Truly it was a different ideal which that finely cultured school of French-Canadian writers, Crémazie, Fréchette, Gérin-Lajoie and others, old now or passed away, had formed for the presentation of the *habitant's* life and ways in *Les Soirées Canadiennes* of forty years ago. Prose of Bernardin de Saint Pierre and verse modelled on Lamartine and the early Hugo, where be ye now? Yet a touch of nature is worth all the culture in the world for popular poetry, and one has only to see an Ontario audience listening to Dr. Drummond's simple but effective way of reciting his poems to understand that, for the English Canadian at least, that language has the stamp of reality and carries with it a true suggestion of the *habitant's* life and character. In its way, therefore, it is a living language, and may be classed with the German-English of Hans Breitmann and the Chicago-Irish of Mr. Dooley as an artistic form of one of those new vernaculars which have arisen in the widely spread territories of the Anglo-Saxon race.

The true Canadian poet will be he who manages to get the right materials of Canadian life into his song in such a way that all the world may feel what it is that gives Canada character and significance amongst nations. I do not mean that we need any more heroic odes on Canada, or celebrations of Lundy's Lane or Chrysler's Farm, but rather a kind of poetry which is able to present the vital features of Canadian life in ordinary scenes and incidents which we recognise with pride and tenderness as distinctively national. It all lies in that "pride and tenderness." That has always, of course, been the line of the great popular or national poet, and nothing less popular seems capable of catching the ear of the democracy of our time. It is not absolutely necessary to be dramatic in form in order to do this. The lyric or descriptive poet has many means of doing it. When Burns sings:

> The boat rocks at the pier o' Leith,
> The wind blaws loud frae ower the ferry,

it is only a farewell song, but it twines into itself characteristic threads of Scottish life and some memories which are deep-seated in the hearts of the poet's countrymen. The Scot can see that little boat rocking at the wet steps of the old stone pier and hear that cold northern blast whistling through the rigging of the emigrant brig in the roadstead, and the chances are it minds him of more than one Willie or Tammas that he is not like to see again. At least it meant all that to the Scot of fifty years ago, and something of the power of its appeal remains with us still. But of course it would be vain for the poet of Ontario or Nova Scotia to try and wake those old chords in the same way. It would even be vain for him to use that language and its cadences, or any modification of that "rustic, hamely jingle" of old Scotia which was so powerful an instrument in the hands of Burns. The poetry of that hardy, self-taught Canadian Scot, Alexander McLachlan, for example, is sincerely enough felt. But though his subjects are Canadian pictures of pioneer farming and the like, his peculiarly Scotch strain, with its pathos, its reverence and its radicalism all so distinctively Scotch, does not make any universal appeal to Canadian readers except as the faint echo of an old song. It can never interpret the spirit and character of the modern democracies of to-day. It is too pathetically naive and tender for that, too much burdened with the sense of a past which is no longer a vital element in the Canadian consciousness.

At present, however, Mr. Roberts seems to have no further thoughts of a Canadian idyll, as far as his poetry, at least, is concerned, but to be moving in the different direction of *New York Nocturnes* and Rossetti's *Worship of Beauty*. Bye and bye, I suppose we shall have airs from the *New Mysticism* of Miss Fionna Macleod and the Celtic School. Of course there is poetry enough to be found in any aspect of life. But its true quality will be extracted only by him who seriously devotes his

51

life to it. Poetry which is drawn from any lesser depth is necessarily imitative in its type and of secondary value. Roberts, like some other of our contemporary writers, needs a sterner literary conscience and more respect for his public. His work belongs too much to the region of artistic experiment. His constant transformations, too, and the ethical heterogeneity of his work take away something of the impression of sincerity and depth which true poetry ought to give us, and which some, at least, of Mr. Roberts' poetry is capable of giving us.

But it is much too soon to write Finis in any estimate of Mr. Roberts' work. He has the true singing quality; and the want of ethical centre and grasp, which has been his weakness hitherto, is one which the years may mend, perhaps, more easily than anything else.